MAJOR M TOURS

AN ADVENTURE & COLORING BOOK

KRISTI TRIMMER

AlaskaWildandFree.com
KristiTrimmer.com

Copyright © 2021 Kristi Trimmer
All rights reserved.
ISBN: 978-1-7369839-0-4

Major Marine Tours is an award-winning, locally-owned Alaska boat tour company celebrating almost 30 years of sharing authentic Alaska adventures with our guests.

In addition to providing world-class customer service, Major Marine Tours is committed to giving back to the community and promoting environmental responsibility through philanthropic giving, partnerships with local non-profit organizations, and performing environmentally-friendly practices on our vessels.

ALASKAN OWNED. OPERATED. LOVED.

Many of us call Alaska home and we are dedicated to supporting the communities that help support us. We are committed to protecting Alaska's wildlife and landscapes so we can continue sharing Alaska's grandeur and beauty with our guests.

Adventure Green Alaska is a voluntary certification program for tourism businesses that meet standards of economic, environmental and social sustainability.

Whale SENSE is an education and recognition program that recognizes whale watching companies committed to responsible practices.

Major Marine Tours was honored by TripAdvisor for the 2020 Travelers' Choice Award for the top travel experiences earning consistently positive reviews.

(907) 224-8030   I   1412 4th Ave., Seward, Alaska 99664   I   majormarine.com

TABLE OF CONTENTS

1. Major Marine Boat
2. Alaska Word Search
3. Bald Eagle
4. Brown Bear
5. Dall's Porpoise
6. Gray Whale
7. Halibut + Salmon
8. Forget Me Knots & Fireweed Flowers
9. Harbor Seal on Ice
10. Hummingbird
11. Humpback Whale
12. Jellyfish
13. Octopus
14. Orca Whales
15. Puffin Rock
16. Sea Otter Maze
17. Starfish
18. Steller Sea Lion Rock
19. Thick Billed Murre
20. Resurrection Bay Map

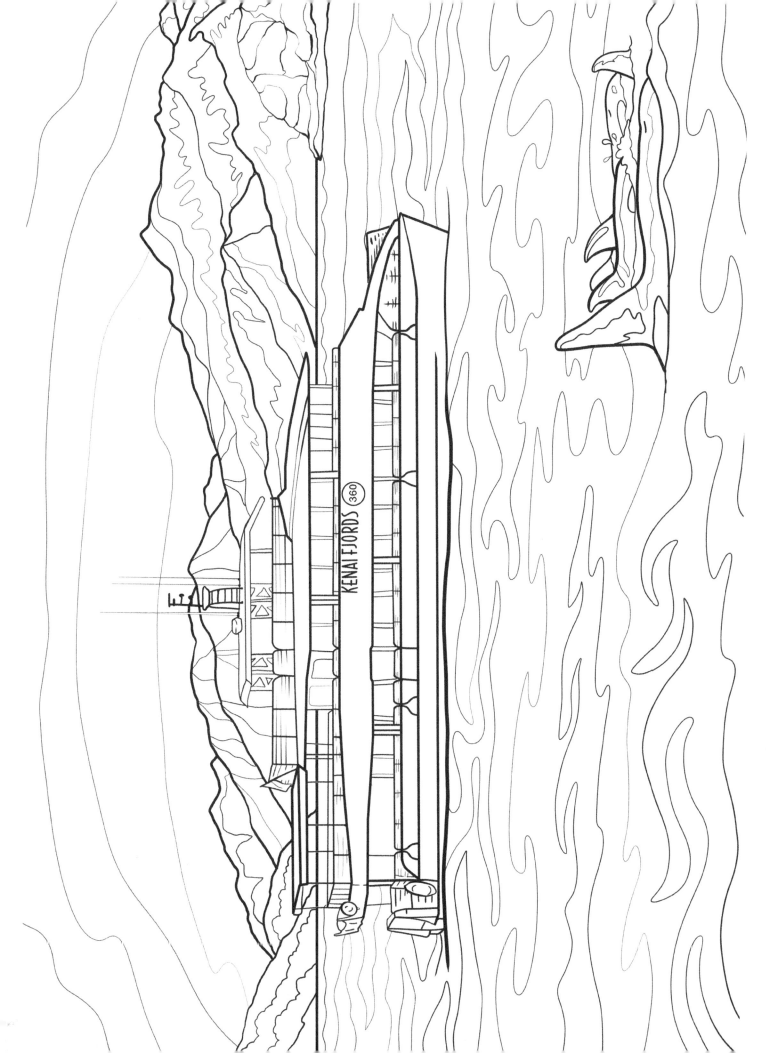

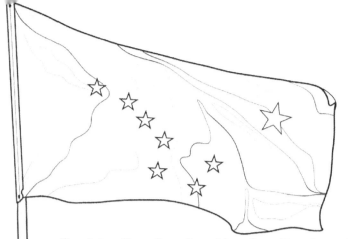

Alaska Word Search

```
S V P A R N O I L A E S R E L L E T S K
Q R P U Z E Y B Z L F K P A W K S O W E
E J E O L H I X Q X F Q A R D L G O Z X
N I W W R Y Q C S N I F F U P A P Q E S
F T X B O P U H A Y O E I T J E R Q W B
J U U I R L O B F L Z J Q K P S H N T F
I W V W C F F I E A G L E D C R L H X V
T X E Y A B P F S A S R E T T O A E S H
B M L N S A G L P E R R A Y U B U P E S
L L B V I B B L R P E J E Y J R I Q W I
A K U H K R W B X H C Z F Z W A N V A F
V P P Q N B A L N T U B I L A H T S R Y
D R I B G N I M M U H A Y B U A A P D L
F W V S T K N O R G X V B M N O P L U L
C V W Y F D W N B O K G P T K G J B E E
I B L X O W P O J D J B D B D Z N F I J
C K K E I B Z M O J A A R G T T I V O S
L U A F Z Z V L Z C P L M T A K S A L A
C O L P X B L A K Y W K G H J U H E K
H S I F R A T S J I Q B Z Q G Q S Z W D
```

Alaska	Gray Whale	Jellyfish	Salmon
Bear	Halibut	Major Marine	Sea Otters
Eagle	Harbor Seal	Orcas	Seward
Flowers	Hummingbird	Porpoise	Starfish
Glacier	Humpbacks	Puffins	Steller Sea Lion

Bald Eagle

Brown Bear

Dall's Porpoise

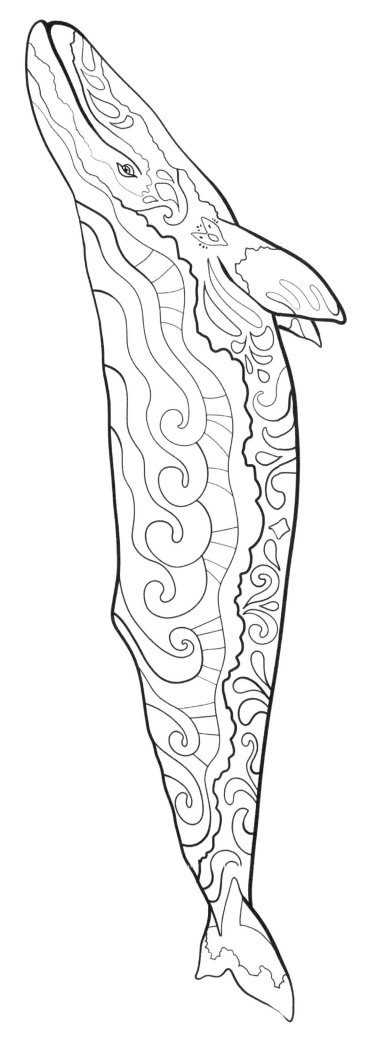
Gray Whale

Harbor Seal at Tidewater Glacier

Hummingbird

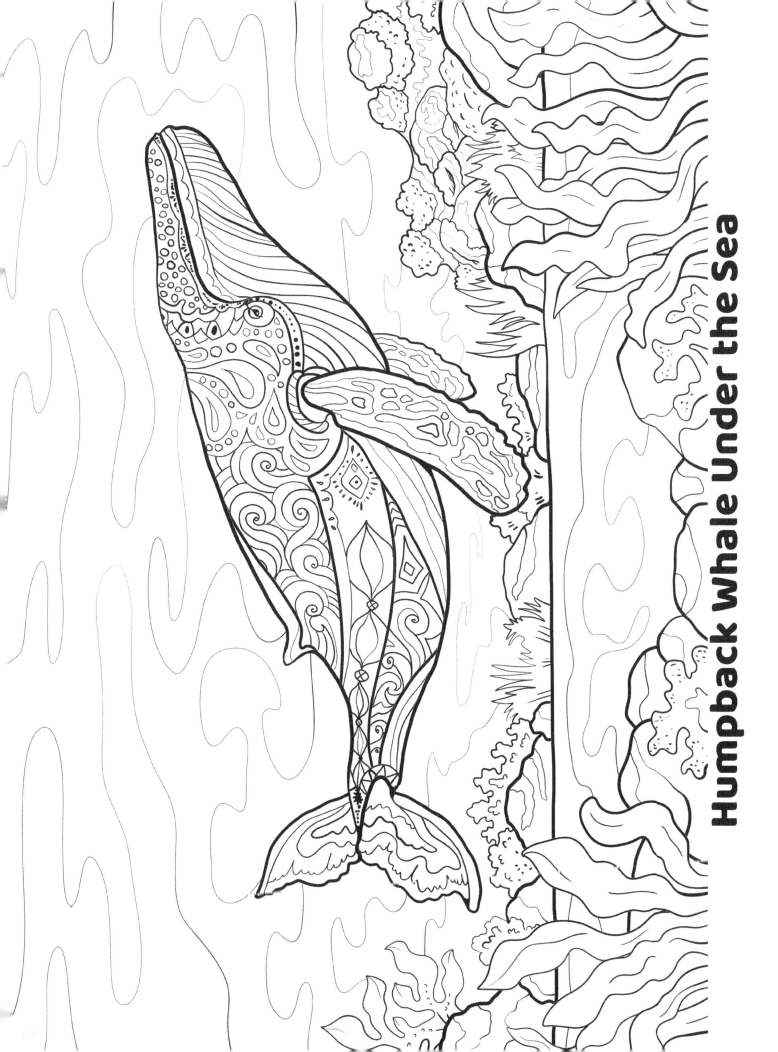
Humpback Whale Under the Sea

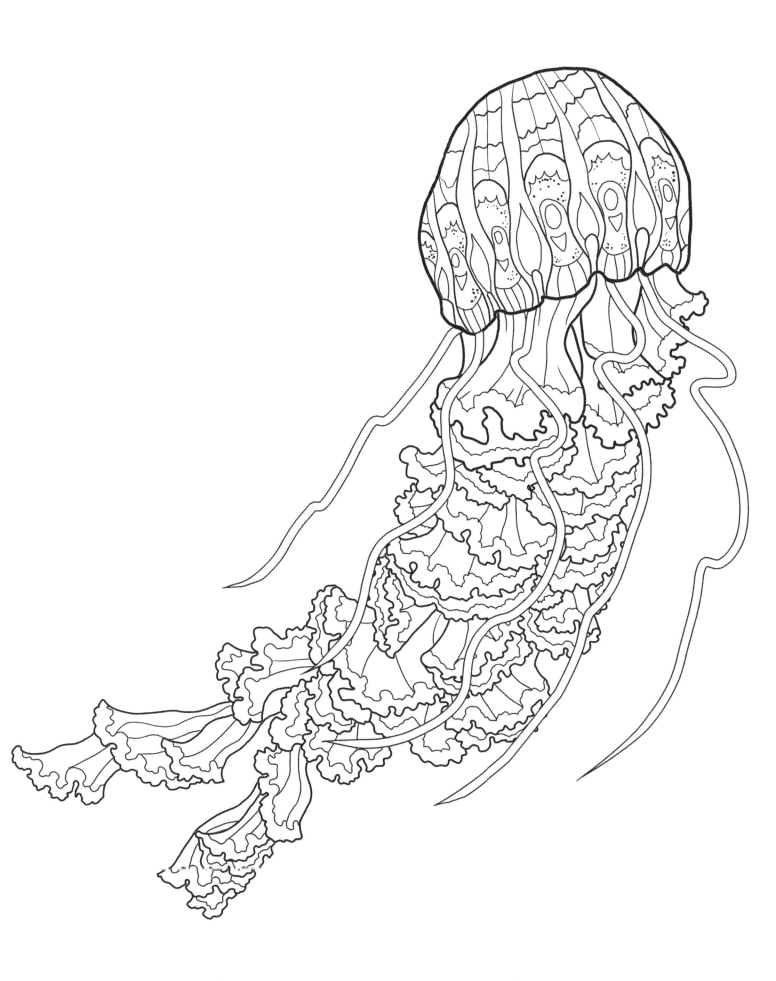

Tiger Mane Jellyfish

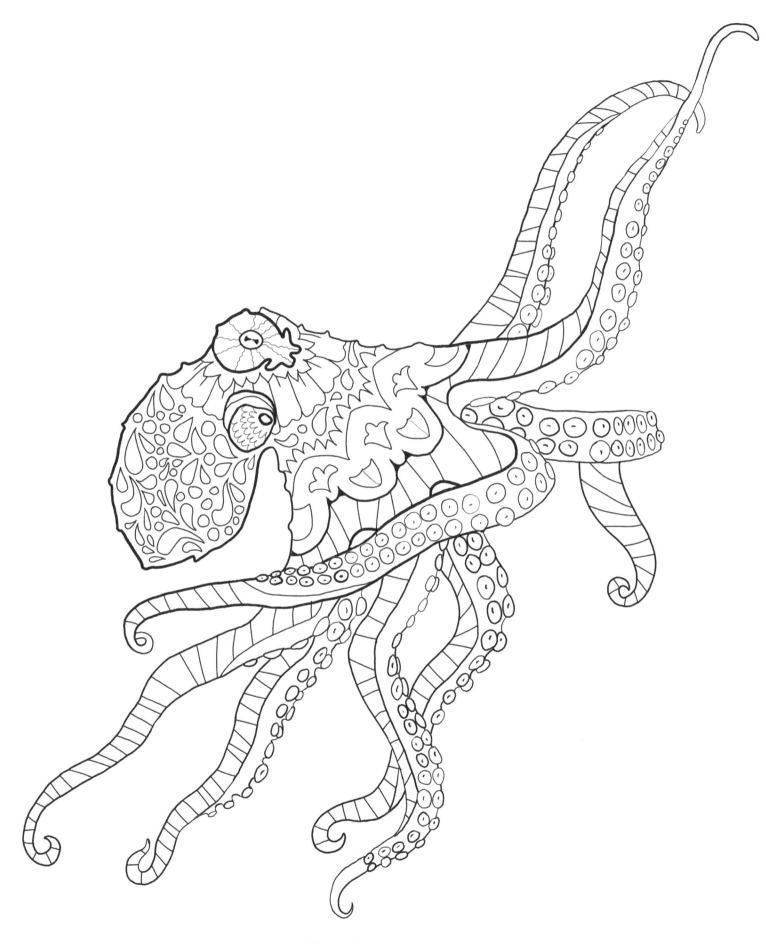

Octopus

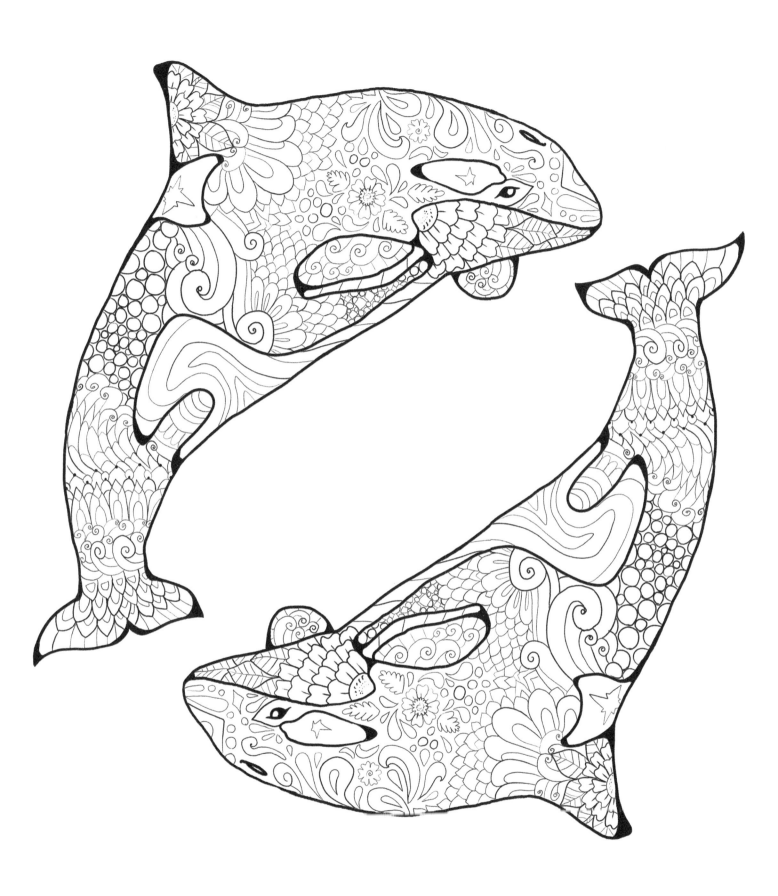

Orca Whales

Horned Puffin + Tufted Puffin

Sea Otter Maze

Starfish

Steller Sea Lion Rock

Thick Billed Murre

It is quite serendipitous to see the photographs I took as I traveled through Alaska come to life as coloring pages in this book. I've taken countless day cruises into Resurrection Bay out of Seward, Alaska, with Major Marine Tours. I had the pleasure to see these magnificent animals enjoying a beautiful Alaska day out on the water. Purely magical!

I spent four years solo camping in National Parks throughout the U.S. as a travel writer. Never in my wildest dreams did I think my six-week adventure to Alaska would result in loving this state so much that I moved here. I'm an Alaska artist and writer, and I absolutely love it.

Alaska is my muse, her beauty my playground.

Follow my Alaska and travel adventures at KristiTrimmer.com and find stickers and magnets that match these illustrations at AlaskaWildandFree.com.

Thank you to my family and friends for supporting me as I've lived this life that is a little less ordinary, and a little bit more wild and free.

Made in the USA
Middletown, DE
19 April 2021